This book is dedicated to

THINKING

Unfortunately, most of man's thinking is in *black* and *white* and rarely ever gets into the

gray matter.

More **MAD** Humor from **SIGNET**

MAD's DAVE BERG LOOKS AT MODERN THINKING

WRITTEN AND ILLUSTRATED BY

DAVE BERG

EDITED BY ALBERT B. FELDSTEIN

Foreword by
Jerry De Fuccio

A SIGNET BOOK from
NEW AMERICAN LIBRARY
TIMES MIRROR
The New English Library Limited, London
New York and Scarborough, Ontario

SIGNET TRADEMARK REG. U.S. PAT. OFF. AND FOREIGN COUNTRIES
REGISTERED TRADEMARK—MARCA REGISTRADA
HECHO EN CHICAGO, U.S.A.

SIGNET, SIGNET CLASSICS, MENTOR, PLUME AND MERIDIAN BOOKS
are published *in the United States* by
The New American Library, Inc.,
1301 Avenue of the Americas, New York, New York 10019,
in Canada by The New American Library of Canada Limited,
81 Mack Avenue, Scarborough, 704, Ontario,
in the United Kingdom by the New English Library Limited,
Barnard's Inn, Holborn, London, E.C. 1, England.

FIRST PRINTING, NOVEMBER, 1969

6 7 8 9 10 11 12 13

PRINTED IN THE UNITED STATES OF AMERICA

FOREWORD . . . MARCH!

Dave Berg was a war correspondent.

Though he received his honorable discharge long ago, Dave still engages in everyday conflicts and continues the war of nerves, yours and ours.

Dave says that life is a beachhead, so you must establish it!

Dave says life is taking the high ground, so you must rise to it!

Dave says life is a rear guard action, so you must go out gracefully!

Yes, Dave Berg is still a war correspondent.

Joyce Kilmer, he's not!

Jerry De Fuccio

**Jerry De Fuccio
Associate Editor**

MUDDLED THINKING

My mother and father **hate** me. They love my sister more. They're always buying her things, like **glasses** and **braces on her teeth** and **corrective shoes**. An' they never buy me **nothin'**.

9

IT'S WHAT'S UP FRONT THAT COUNTS

11

13

SOUND OFF

17

POUND CAKE

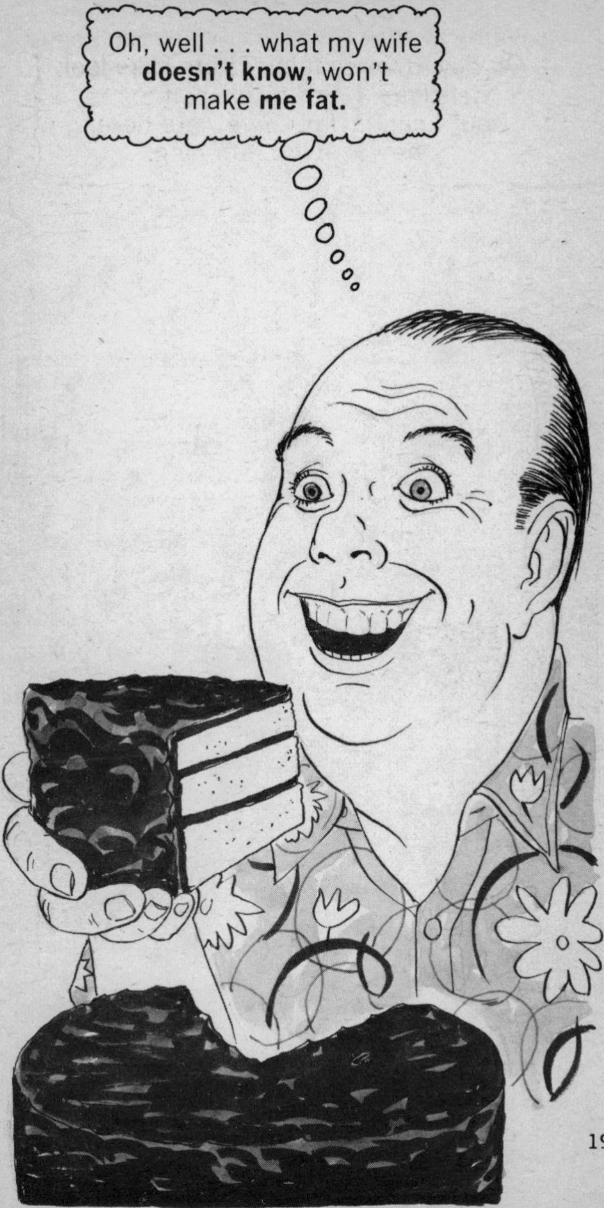
Oh, well . . . what my wife **doesn't know,** won't make **me fat.**

LOVE FINDS A WAY

21

23

THE BURNING QUESTION

Gee, those poor women. Their apartment house is on fire and they had to get out in a hurry in the middle of the night. I can just imagine what horrible thoughts are going through their minds right now.

29

LOVE IS PATERNAL

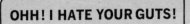

VOX POP

37

A GROWING PAIN

40

41

43

BRUSH OFF

46

THE YEAHS HAVE IT

CLASS DISTINCTION

DOCTOR H.
SARATOGA

54

55

KID NAPPING

59

SEEN BUT NOT HURT

63

SLIGHT OF HAND

69

71

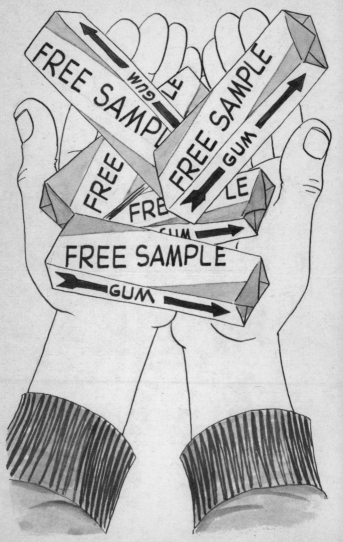

SOCIAL THINKING

NAME DROPPER

Whenever I'm under a pressure situation,
I forget people's names.
Like when I'm being a hostess, and I
have to introduce everybody to everybody,
then my mind suddenly goes blank.

FOOT IN MOUTH DISEASE

If there's anything I can't stand,
it's an embarrassing silence.

79

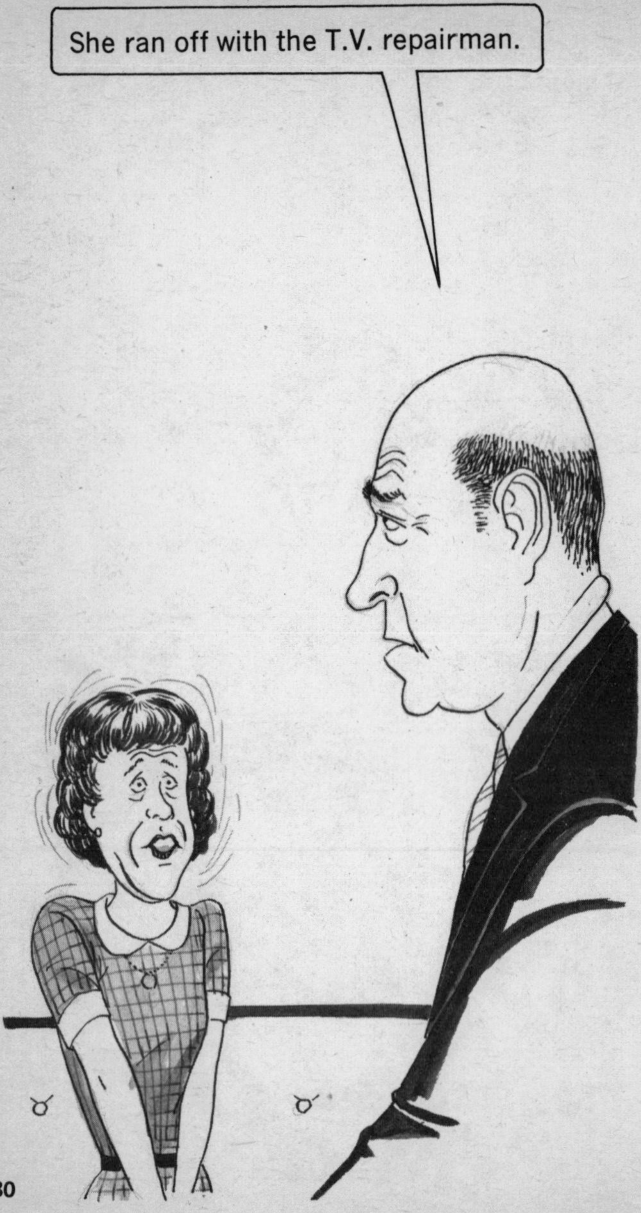
She ran off with the T.V. repairman.

If there's anything I can't stand, it's an embarrassing conversation.

CURLING IRONY

GET UNACQUAINTED

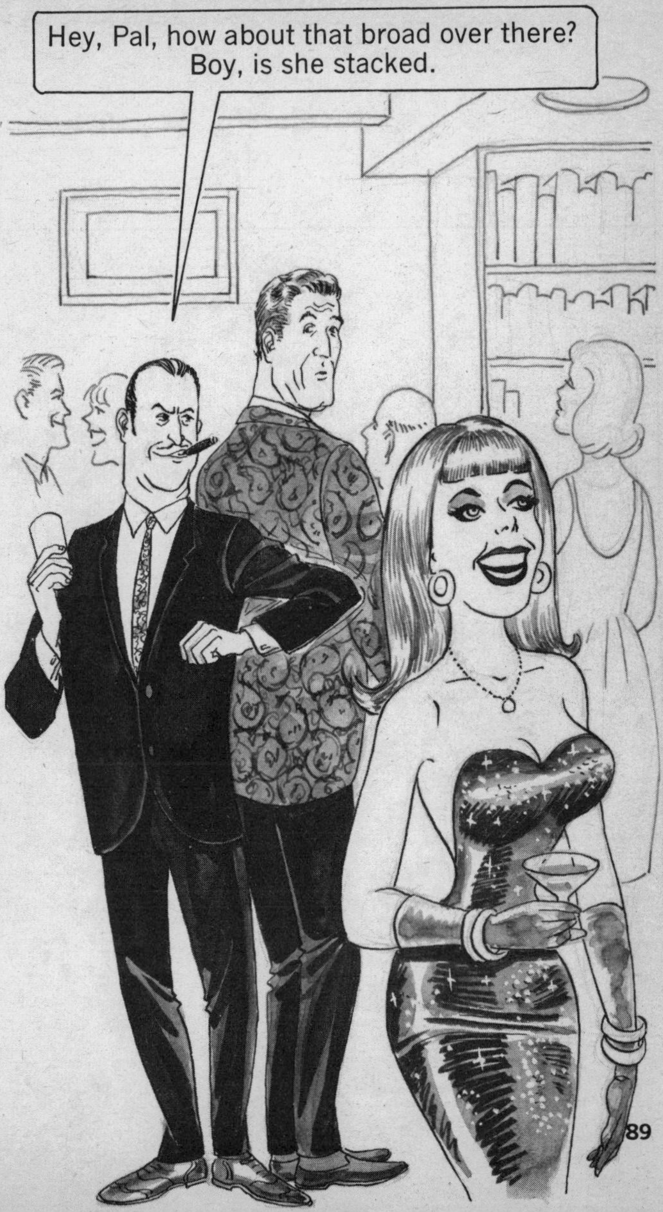
Hey, Pal, how about that broad over there?
Boy, is she stacked.

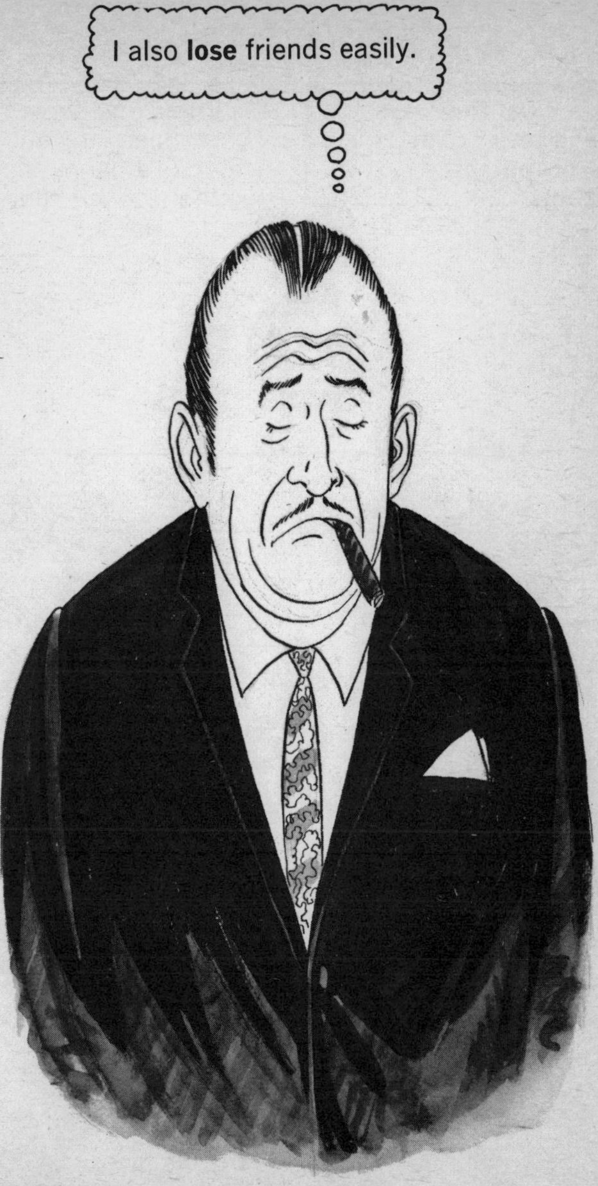
I also **lose** friends easily.

PARTY PEPPER

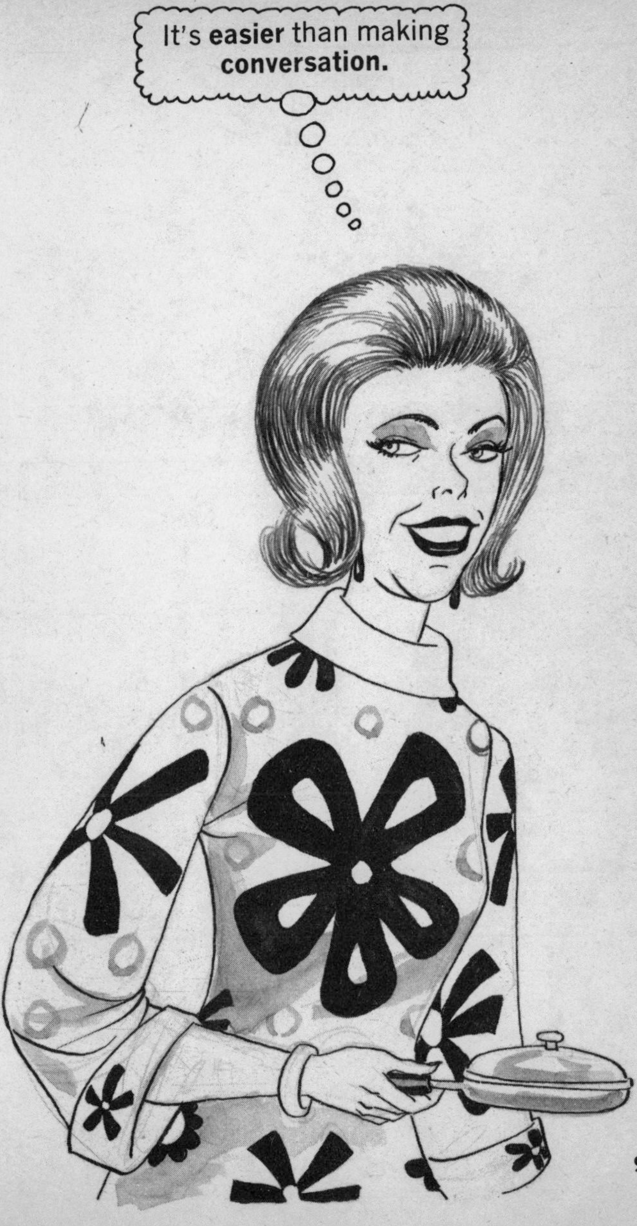
It's **easier** than making **conversation.**

DON'T COME AS YOU ARE

SENSUAL THINKING

SWITCH HITTER

LINE - O - TYPE

I'd like to have a harem of 80 beautiful scanty clad wives. Each one at my beck and call . . .

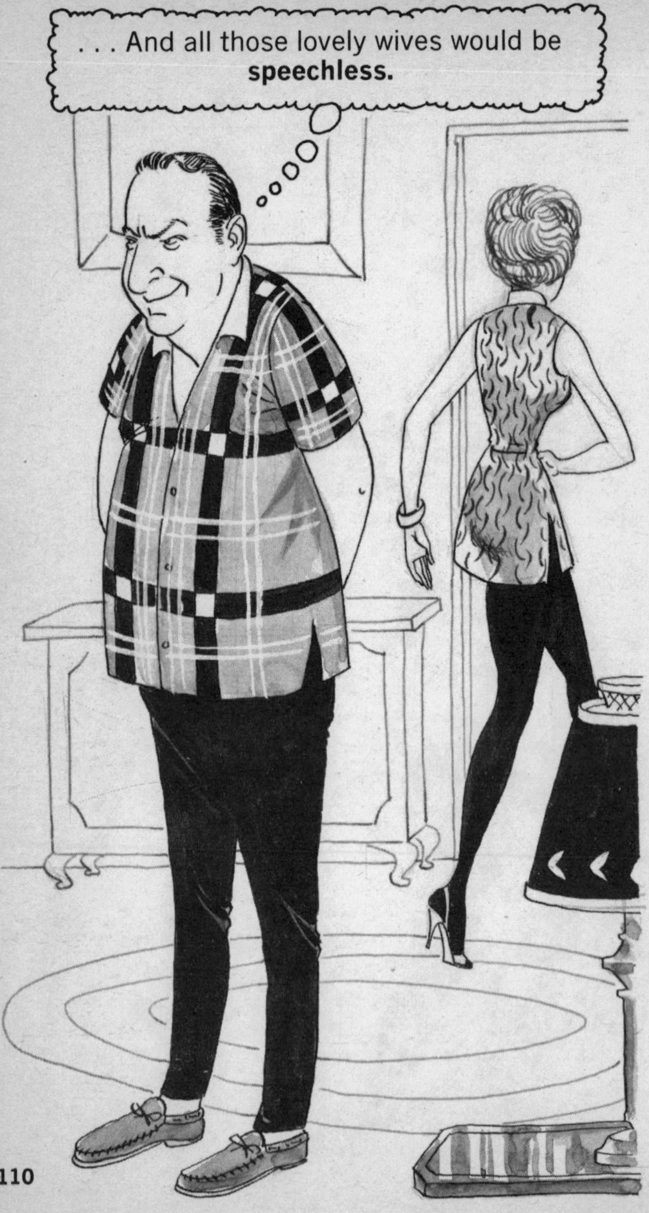
. . . And all those lovely wives would be **speechless.**

WIN, PLACE AND SHOW

I got it! I'll take her to McDonald's to eat. All the guys hang around that hamburger joint. Then I can show her off.
EH 7615

Imagine taking me to a cheap hamburger joint. That's the last time this slob will be seen with me.

THE NOSE KNOWS

Look at those girls wearing bikinis. They are teasingly hiding what in our society is considered **sexy.** In primitive societies, women go around with nothing on but body paint. Yet their men aren't in a constant state of passion.

As I understand it, in Japan, it's the **back of a woman's neck** that's supposed to drive men wild.

117

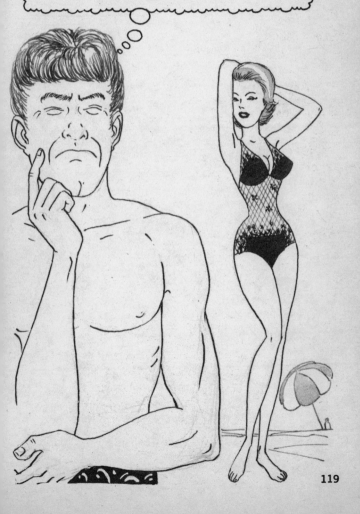

Furthermore, **nose jobs** would no longer consist of **reducing** the size but rather **enlarging** it with **silicone.** And women, to show modesty, would teasingly wear **nose bras.** Small nosed women would wear padded ones, and young girls would wear **training** nose bras.

PHILOSOPHICAL THINKING

PUTTING DESCARTES BEFORE THE HORSE

Come to think about it, how do I know anything? Is everything really as it seems to be? How do I know I'm actually me? Maybe I'm just a bad dream somebody is having.

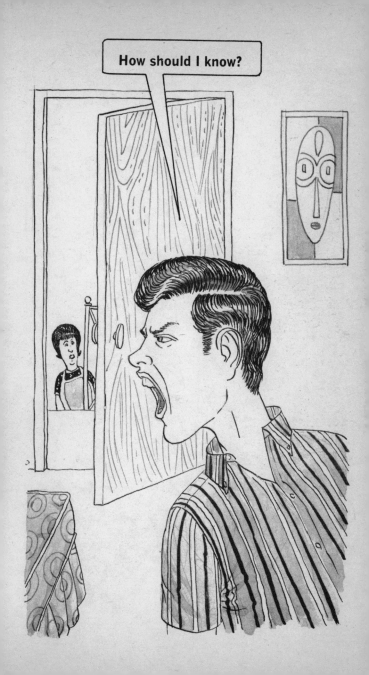

LOVE MAKES THE WORLD GO FLAT

127

128

THERE'S THE RIB

My mother says she's got hang-ups because her mother did—so did her grandmother. Like it's an inheritance passed on from one generation to another going all the way back to Eve.

There's just one trouble with this whole theory.

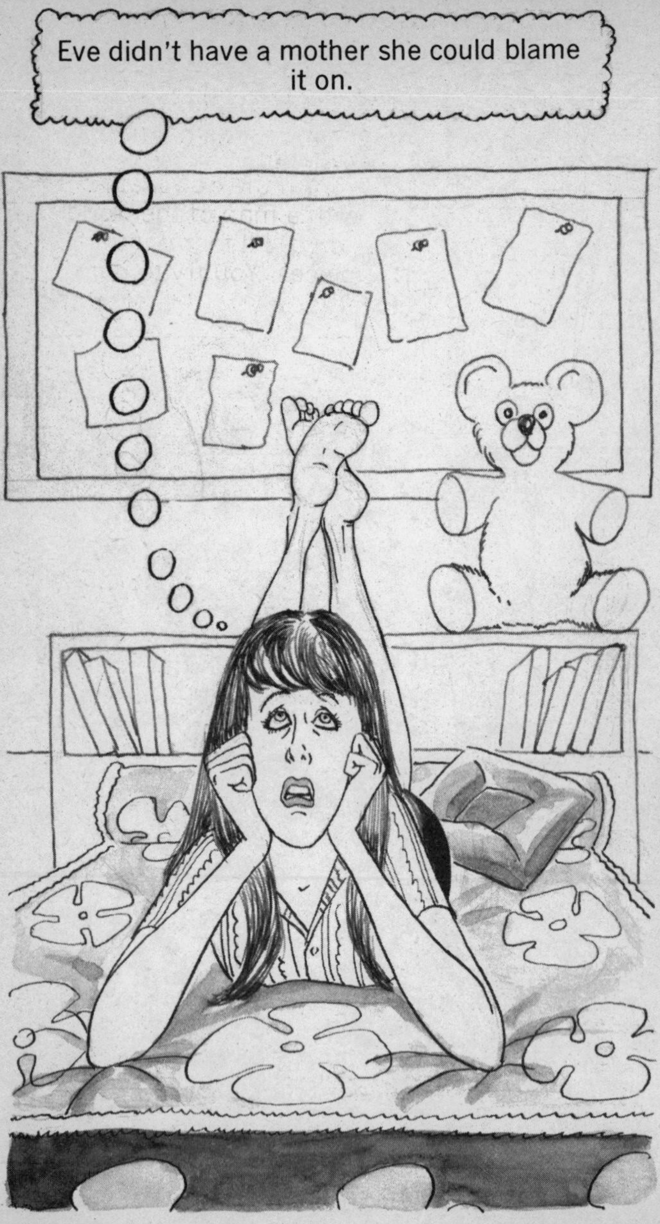
Eve didn't have a mother she could blame it on.

TURN-ABOUT IS FAIR PLAY

That should keep him off my back for a couple of hours. Especially with the complicated mess the world is in, he'll probably never figure it out.

135

GOODNESS KNOWS

How do I **know** there's a **God?** I never **saw** Him. And another thing, who **made** God? And who made the **maker** of God? And what was there **before** the beginning? And where does the universe **end?** And what's on the **other side?**

138

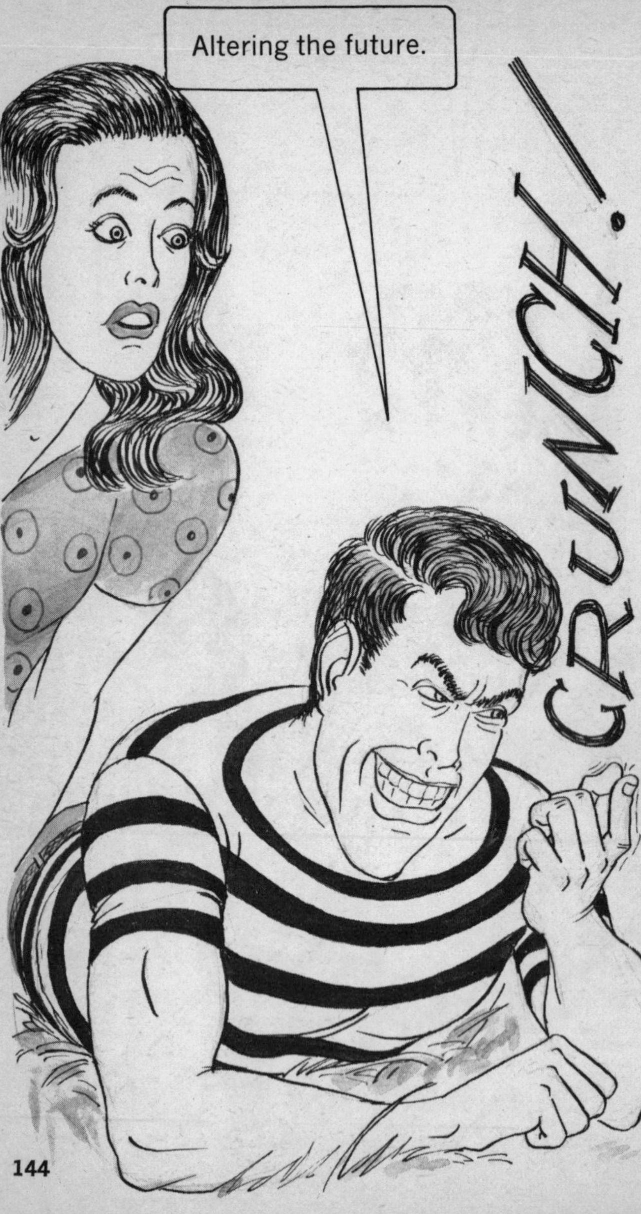
Altering the future.
CRUNCH!

HYPOCRITICAL THINKING

SUNNY DISPOSITION

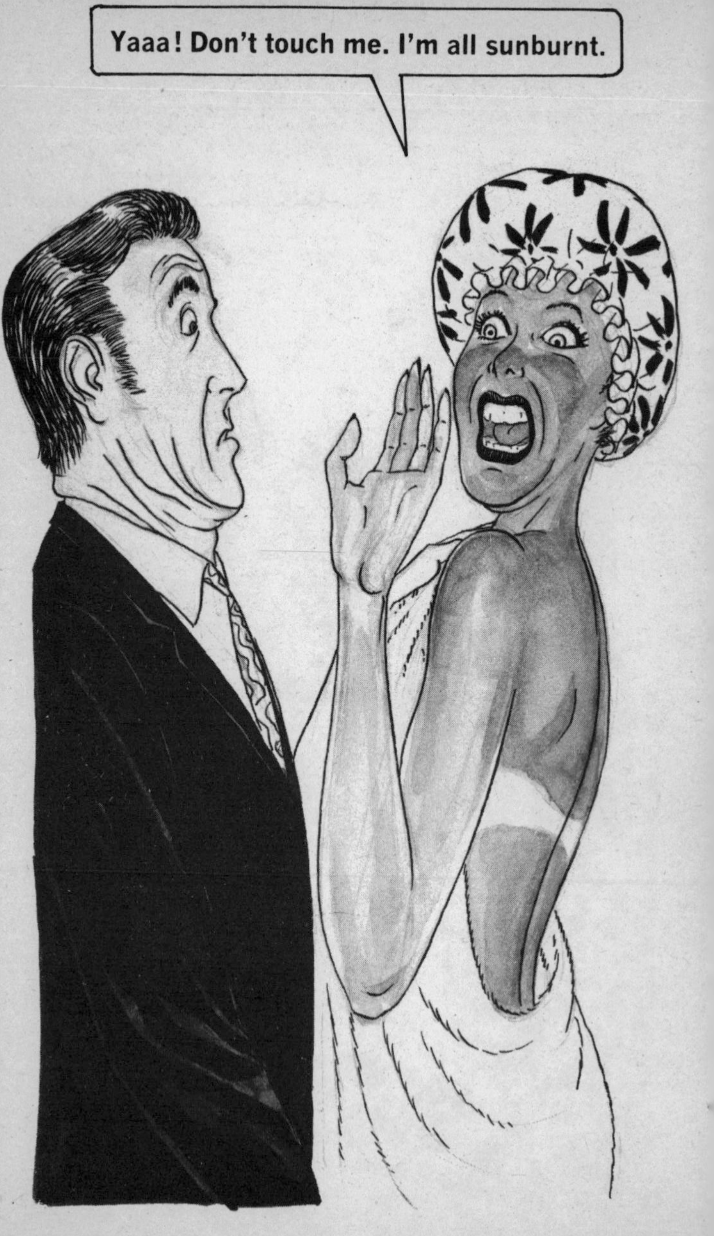
Yaaa! Don't touch me. I'm all sunburnt.

BUDDY SYSTEM

THE JOKER IS MILD

Hey, I heard this gag. A man asks his wife if she knows Beethoven. So she says, "Sure I do, I saw him just this morning on the A bus going down Main Street." So he says **"Stupid,** if you don't know what you're talking about then **shut up!** You're only making a fool of yourself. Anybody knows that the **A Bus doesn't** go down Main Street."

FEAT OF CLAY

I mean it.

Look, I'm an ordinary guy, no better, no worse than anyone else. I have my faults, my pettiness, my jealousies like any other mortal.

So don't go building me up to something I can't live up to.

That's another quality about you that I love, your **modesty.**

THE CUSTOMER IS ALWAYS RIGHTEOUS

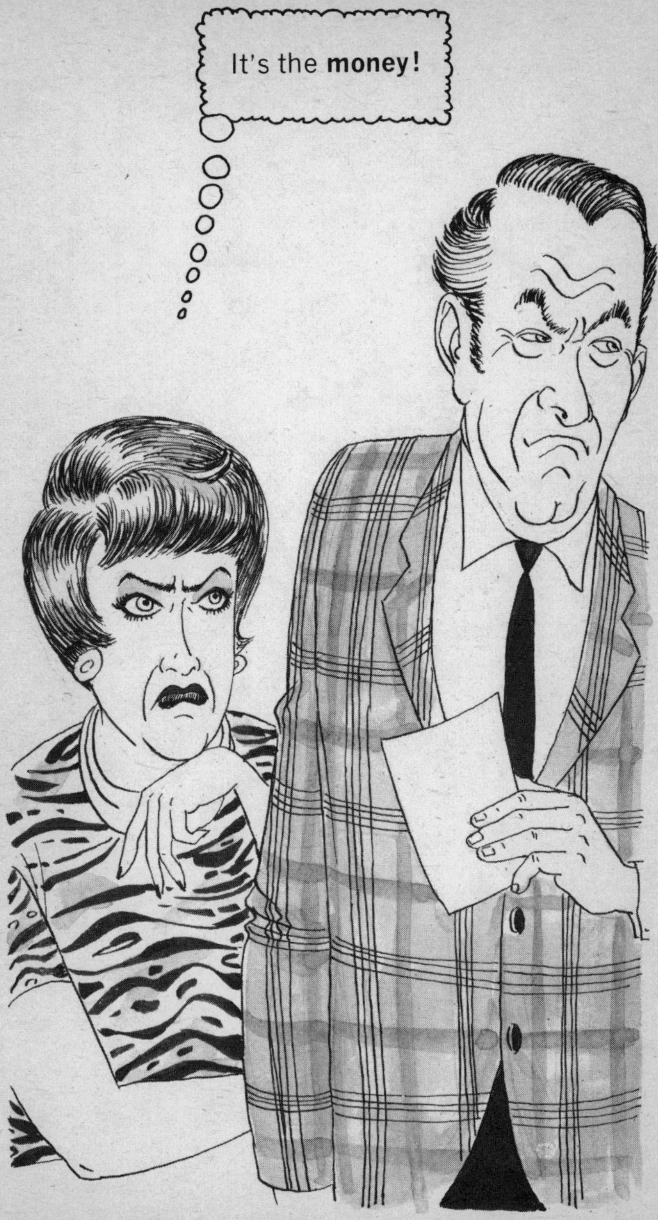
It's the **money**!

TIME OF HIS WIFE

167

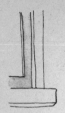

TOM
ZARETSKY
THE GREAT

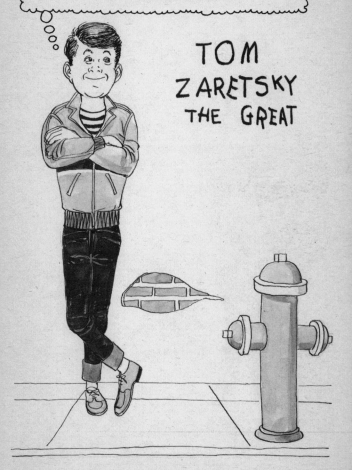

LAUNDROMATE

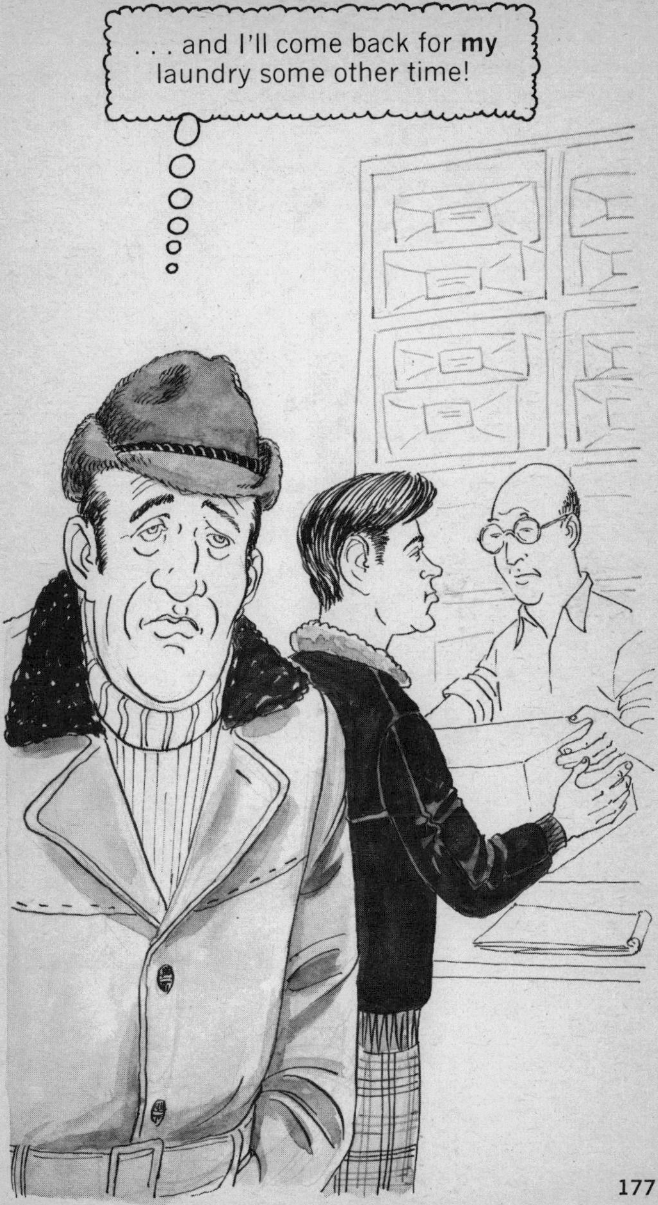
. . . and I'll come back for **my** laundry some other time!

BEGGARS CAN BE LOSERS

180

183

184

SUNDAY KIND OF LOVE

HEX MARKS THE SPOT

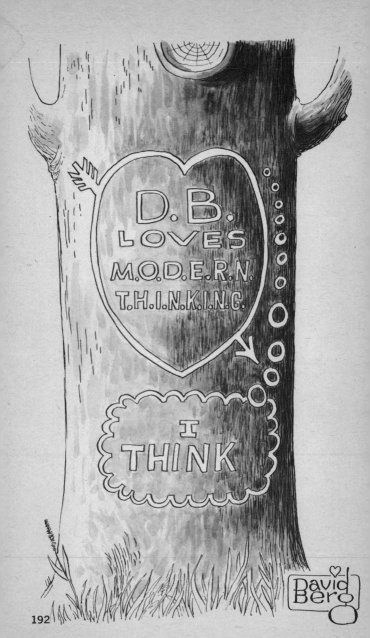